To Howard & M[illegible]
With fond wishes
Saul

MY DAD WAS NOT HAMLET

SAUL LANDAU

Institute for Policy Studies
Washington, D.C.

Institute for Policy Studies
1601 Connecticut Avenue
Washington, D.C. 20009

Manufactured in the United States of America

Library of Congress Cataloging-in-Publication Data

Cover Photo: Haskell Wexler
Cover Design: Ross A. Feldner of New Age Graphics

ISBN: 0-89758-049-4 (paper) $9.95

First Edition

93-79745
CIP

OTHER WORKS BY SAUL LANDAU

BOOKS

The New Radicals (with Paul Jacobs)

To Serve the Devil (with Paul Jacobs)

Assassination on Embassy Row (with John Dinges)

The Dangerous Doctrine:
National Security and U.S. Foreign Policy

Guerrilla Wars of Central America:
Nicaragua, El Salvador & Guatemala

FILMS

Fidel

Brazil: Report on Torture (with Haskell Wexler)

¿Que Hacer?

The Jail

The CIA Case Officer (with Haskell Wexler)

Paul Jacobs and the Nuclear Gang (with Jack Willis)

Quest for Power: Sketches of the American New Right
(with Frank Diamond)

Target Nicaragua (with Haskell Wexler)

The Uncompromising Revolution

FOR SAUL

His poems limp (this is not a derogatory term of literary criticism but a question of being true; here to limp is to arrive wounded, with one's self-respect intact) his poems limp, use the telephone booths reserved for the handicapped, walk with a white stick and black glasses, wait at the curb in a wheelchair, use the sign language of the deaf and dumb, have an empty sleeve tucked into the side pocket, crawl on their elbows if necessary, and continually remember those who disappeared.

He plays raquetball, enjoys baseball, runs, knows the quickest way to the airport, can write a national newspaper column in 50 minutes, reserves the best table in a restaurant when he wants to give pleasure to a friend, and wears white socks.

When do they meet then, the poems and the poet? They meet often. Once or twice a week over many years they've met. They are alone when they meet, very alone, poem on the paper, man with his eyes shut and his brows creased.

Equally, they are not alone. The place they meet is packed with those whom the present has forgotten and those who are not booked for the future. These people look up when the poet comes through the door from the street. They recognise him, but they resume their forever unfinished conversations. He writes on the back of an envelope. Often he writes standing up, or half sitting, half leaning on the corner of a table.

Where is it? On a corner by the next set of lights. Where the Pet Names of loved ones across the History of the Twentieth Century. From street level you go down a stairway, then left to where you see figures standing by a bar. Many have walked out from there to their deaths. There's a lot of pain and you hear laughter.

Everything spoken is in an unknown language and every back is turned. This is why he has to write in the hope that the poem will turn its head and address him by name.

Of course all poems (not only his) are about pain. One can plan utopias in prose, never in poetry. Whatever their subjects, poems are also about time passing and the little that is left. Yet poetry affirms. Miraculously affirms. How?

They know the answer to this question in the bar on the corner, but they're not telling.

Language listens to poetry. And so there's recognition, not of gain or prestige but of loss and affliction. Some of the pain is shared and in the sharing there is a promise of rebecoming part of a whole.

The poems on the envelopes walk the poet (and us) home.

John Berger
July, 1993

INTRODUCTION

"*Je suis un autre*" said Rimbaud. This refers to the revelation of the "other" that all of us, like Rimbaud, carry within ourselves. I've always thought of this "other" as the poet, the one who presides in and celebrates the light within the heart of darkness itself.

That a man has hidden, during his years of adolescence, youth and maturity his work in the light in order to give his strength, his imagination and his sensitivity to dismal endeavors, that is the work of a poet.

Saul Landau has diverse vocations — writer, filmmaker, professor; a man devoted to matters of domestic and foreign policy; a man with a clear calling to change life.

This "other" that has accompanied him through the years, has been served by poetry, the guardian angel that has enabled him to devote himself to work for vital change; efforts that demand almost total dedication; activity that require an enormous dose of optimism.

I do not think it is presumptuous to say that Landau has looked at his surroundings with eyes of love and tenderness, and has seen nature and its creatures exposed to the ravages of time and its agents; and to the damage inflicted by human impiety. Otherwise, the verses you are about to read would not have been written. Landau has converted love and tenderness into weapons of daily combat against pain and fear, uncertainty, loss of passion, fatigue and the other maladies afflicting the end of this century. Publicly, Landau struggles against them, secretly he exorcises them through poetry.

His attitude reminds me of Ruben Martinez de Villena, a poet who preferred to give his life to the fight to "change life" for others rather than to nurture the gifts of his spirit. Martinez Villena sacrificed his poetic work in response to the indifference of many toward social justice. Fortunately, his published poems were saved for the glory of Spanish language poetry.

That Landau publishes his work and shares it with those who are publicly and secretly nourished by poetry is an act of generosity that we should joyously celebrate.

Landau revives those universal and eternal themes that poets have always addressed, from Pindar and Homer to Lowell and Ginsberg: the mother as the center of the personal universe and the relationship with her from the days of infancy; the family, friendship, home life and the immense effort of some men and women to make human that which remains habitable in this world; contemporary life in society, whose contradictions and antagonisms threaten constantly all that exists, the irredeemable passing of time and seasons, like life and death.

These are his themes, but how does he approach and define them? Exactly as the poets do, with words. But his words gather together and captivate after leaving their mark on our consciousness. His words strike. Not with the intention of punishing or mistreating, but rather as a warning, a protest, a prophecy.

Pablo Armando Fernandez

MY DAD WAS NOT HAMLET

TABLE OF CONTENTS

PART 3 ANXIETY IN THE REDWOODS

PART 4 THE AGE OF REVOLUTION —AND PAIN

PART ONE
THE LIVING NEED A POEM

MORNING RHYTHMS

AWAKE

Dawn light leaks
    through venetian blinds
    in the bathroom
where I hear the creaks
of aging wooden boards
    half bath
    not even a bathtub
unpleasant words store
secrets of unspoken capers
    I reflect to escape
    terrifying tales
routine daily paper.

FIRST THOUGHTS

From the window a moving van
    prepares to make history
    I see slender joggers
promise to buy a walkman
I resent my corroding knees
    react to aromas downstairs
    baneful gases of middle age
not dissolved in spring breezes
I respond with whines
    my expectations offended
    immature nasal emotions
not yet ready to resign

NOSTALGIA

Where fresh gardenias' scent prevailed
a musty redolence unveiled
  the wrinkles scarring Helen's lines
    that silky smoothness once defined —
        a face and neck
        of great appeal

BATH

        I stare at rumpled ankles
        testing the climate of the pool
        my cracked foot bottoms
        vulnerable apertures
    to microscopic enemies
        symbols of lost integrity

NOSTALGIA

My affections become engaged
when I discern my very image
    in hazy dawn through filtered sky
    a tenuous grasp on integrity —
    compared to younger surer years

DRESS

Sharp crumbs from morning muffins
    spear loosened threads
woolen sweater reeking
    vapors of anxiety
dried in faded golden weaves
    remains of snowy lambs
lying in deadened red cedar
    oxidized residues

of brown moths and gray larvae,
    ancient mascara flakes upon
fading colors alter textures
    challenge my vision, my flesh

BREAKFAST

No oatmeal in the cupboard
new keys on the key ring
area codes to memorize
accusations toward
unfair cookie allocation
missing hair clasps
barking dog, hunger pains
cloud other sensations

TO WORK

The path of life
    the petty skits
actors
audience
    unable to laugh
  in the face of the wind —
then, the flash from a gray cloud
a phrase,
    a child's expression —
the urge to create.

May 1993

LOSS OF INNOCENCE

I am spring robin
I do not decide
a flight's purpose to
fetch a straw or
fry an egg arrange
a slept-in bed
for thirty-five years I
have torn resistant plastic
seals poured uncounted brown
flakes fried five thousand
eggs I measure Time
in birthday candles loss
of innocence on browned
photos and fuzzy videotapes.

I have not learned
to wait I spread
my weary arms ride
the hostile wind enjoy
the wicked Sun I
water my shoots with
regret beam at blooming
flowers curse licentious weeds
wonder how the child
understood meaning in dinosaurs.

November 1989 — August 1990
as Julia left the hospital.

THE KID IN THE PLAYGROUND

Flowers bloom
with vigor
on the lawn
of the house
where the boy died
suicide
used drugs they said
he had problems
depression
used to smoke
weed
in the school yard
break bottles
on the basketball court
before he left home
for college
where he died
what to say
to grieving parents
cross my fingers
knock on wood
but for the grace of God
twenty years old
amid final exams
was it rejection
some girl
woman these days
he was a man
not quite ready maybe
blooming flowers
have different
sorts of problems
growing up

May 1993

TOO LATE

I worried over Minnesota
did you receive my
belated new year's card
I waited a day
too early isn't good
I wondered what arrangements
meant the kinds you
made and the times
you lay in bed
and read your head
next to my head
I was five or
was I eight instead
of appreciating I demanded
untutored when want and
lust turn and sour
you didn't trust me
how dramatic I am
why trust stupid kids
I was your son
how little you demanded
I erase my ingratitude
I make no pledges
to applaud your sacrifices
over North Dakota gray
no strings attached except
those my mind ties
the jet struggles through
silent clouds and I'm
an orphan at last.

1983

A GRECIAN JOG

I don't leap from
bed, rage forth
to prolong the dawn.
Instead,
I obey
the dreamy
threads of pogroms,
infect caffeine-driven
caprice;
dread the lure
of newly-strewn headlines.

I tug at lower limbs;
integrity
intact, inhale
diesel-flavored breeze;
counteract
demands,
shrieking, puerile fascists,
facts in B flat.
The taunts of provocative crows,
reminders
of synoptic pleas,

creaky brittle,
binding one, two,
cartilage,
three, four;
wind pierces nostrils,
The Count of Monte Cristo
leaps, sword in hand,
finds the maiden;
a fence,
a garden hose,

obligations
suck scarce oxygen.

I exhale,
two, three, gasp,
punji sticks of glass,
slaloms in rutted roads,
fungus between toes,
half thoughts of
half nights,
lazy lungs,
on drooping lines
of Brothers Karamazov
clothes hung,
grinding bones; check watch,

mark time.
Grandpa,
imagine if you
will,
adventurous British Lords
filling bowls with Samian wine,
the appeal of Greeks,
writing a novel;
up hill, eight minute mile!
were there virgins
posed in the shade
of pogroms?

A horn
yells,
dancing gases twirl.
The Bells of St. Mary's
measure morning minutes;
memory-drenched droplets
tell of odysseys,

drip down my drawers;
a well of treadless Nikes,
remnants, undigested yesterdays,
a trace of ancient Gods.

July 1992

T.S. ON YOU, MY YOUTH

(LOOKING BACK AT ELIOT)

I've taken to wearing my trousers flared
No one, I assume, even remotely cares
old friends gone
new ones drift
Singles search or, eventually, they pair.

My thinning hair looks well-groomed short
An excuse I use when due in court
old routines languish
new ones illusive
Patterns, like spider webs, hard to sort.

I still seek seats beside women on planes
Vexation has made my appetite wane
thrills become scarce
pro football bores
People I thought sound have gone rather insane.

I rarely take umbrage over "news" these days
My eyes have adjusted to mist, smog and haze
colors seem dimmer
pornography dull
I dare not predict the next cultural craze.

I still admire Picasso, his nudes and his dove;
I tend to study them from my perch high above
music means less
not Nero Wolfe
I think I pile sandbags on unsatisfied love.

1985

ANCIENT HISTORY

Recall the virtuous raging on streets
a thousand Christs in black and olive green
in distant wilderness, mountains, jungles,
tableaus of haloed saints in battle scenes.

Scraggly beards and long, limp hair
guerrillas setting fashion trend,
in times of Tet, mid rockets glare,
brave new worlds begun — or ended?

October 1991

FANTASY RASH

You smiled
    I broke out in fantasy rash
    my lips erupted
    to cover your mouth
    my toes groped
    for forbidden zones

In my dream
    words flow
    dandruff falls
    shadows strobe
    on papered walls

Little Miss Muffet sits on my mind
whirlpool of refuse in a nursery rhyme
long winter underwear warms as it clings
your pies break open, black birds sing

In an open-air bus
    someone sighs
    someone sneezes
    paper rustles
    winter breezes

I close my eyes
    my cannons bellow, your jets hum
    diving vintage fighters drone
    fragments of God Is My Copilot
    set like jello
    into gray and wrinkled sleep

1988

GETTING THE FLU IN AMSTERDAM

I

I hear accented inflections
bounce off cranky white walls
between elocution and gesture,
a sure omen when temptations
of windows lure me to look at
monumental roof tops and
a purposeful woman tossing
viscous liquid into a backyard
of North Sea gray.

II

Nothing wrong with feeling bad,
I smile, in reaction to an issue,
absorbing invisible waves
of hidden acrimony
accumulated over decades of meetings
in the musty air of
procedures trained to shroud
bilious impulses
in the right angles of a room.

III

Cigarettes, very European still,
emit curls of snaking and writhing
smoke that explode
inside my vulnerable nostrils,
wriggle into dry caverns
of throat and settle comfortably
in the cuddly sacs of my lungs.
An ash falls to the carpet
recherche du temps perdu

IV

A yellowing leaf floats downward,
my spirit droops into dampness,
the Nature of November
in oude Amsterdam where God,
according to the painter,
gave nocturnal orders, a mission,
deprived him of light
to drive him mad to France
— a better place, I'm told.

V

An invisible Meister
sneaks into meeting rooms,
stains the young in sobriety,
camouflages the smoke
cloistered in the pores
of tattered cloth
secure in canvases
of anatomy classes and
Delft from across the stream.

VI

A late November maple leaf
struggles against the wind
on a resolute path;
drafts race across my calves
like icy, ivy fingers;
I try to seal the cracks where
trousers peck at socks;
I clutch my invisible branch
through the window of a meeting.

November 1992

LAST CHRISTMAS BEFORE CASTRO

Peering into the heart of the city from across the Bay was Jesus himself, white, fifty feet high, not really looking, the object of religious oohs and ahs, a leaning post for the soldiers. The dictator had ordered the sculptor to shape and design the face of the Lord to resemble that of *El Presidente's* wife. The sculptor succeeded. The Dictator was pleased and *El Cristo de Habana* was to be unveiled amidst wreaths of flowers and military displays with paunchy generals weighted with U.S. medals, assisted by high Churchmen; the townspeople of Regla and Casa Blanca peered up from their hillside hovels and their goats casually dropped round pellets over the newly-laid terrace that surrounded *El Cristo.*

In the city itself no one took notice. It played no part in the life of the narcotics peddler and international gangster, or the teenage girl learned in the most subtle, aristocratic sex perversions, or her thin mulatto pimp who sold exclusively to the American dolce vita set that found Miami Beach dull. It did not matter to the bitter students hiding in plush apartments, waiting for him to come down from the Sierra. What did it matter that the Tyrant was to unveil a statue of the Lord?

The *Cha Cha Cha* and *Pachanga,* fluted and strummed, filled the bars and clubs, *chistosos* danced with young women, mouths slightly turned down, ass drawn with fine lines by the expensive skirt, round belly tapering off into the essence of Cuba. The Pearl of the Antilles.

Near the docks men glanced at the white object, shuffling rhythmically toward their work, swinging short-sleeved arms, a slight bend in the knees, visible through loose trousers. The Lord was watching the gamut of color, speckled like an action painting, faces, blouses, buildings, tropical flowers, sky and sea, pastels and full reds; smelling from the sweat of the poor, the black, the brown, the shades in between; from hairy legs, freshly showered, lightly-sweating armpits; from the sea, the seaweed, the rotting fish, burning gasoline.

Around the majestic statue were old toothless women, some with functions, others landmarks, dried and wise, the wisdom of a thousand abortions in their eyes, their hands the victims of grease from the primitive kitchens and oil from smooth-skinned babies; they had absorbed the juices of many bodies rubbed together, their hands placed on a black-covered knee, hawking, shouting commands, advice to the shoeshine boys and professional car parkers. They shared their city with the tourists, the gamblers, the whores, businessmen and servants — all family.

"*Que monstruoso.* Look at the size. I hear that it is El Cristo."

A laugh, a smile, a nod at the priest who saw sex and sin written indelibly into the wrinkles and mustaches of all over twenty. The *cura* knew that these *Cubanos* had seen the inside, the mystery of the human canals, had squeezed the fruits of pleasure and then watched their own fluids drained for the fuel that kept the sick mechanism smiling. It had been a baptism of fifty years of American tourists, an initiation into obstetrics, peering into the wombs of aborted Miami society. Those that were fighting, hiding, playing war could not get that smell off their hands, but this too could be accepted with a smile. What difference that a great edifice to the Lord would watch from across the harbor?

From the huts of Regla and Casa Blanca, they emerged, slowly creeping up the hillside toward the white Lord. The red-shirted, red-skirted young with low-cut blouse, old with chickens, pigs and skinny dogs with open mouths, pouring from their *Bembe*-soaked shacks, dark faces, wide eyes. The cult murderers in black pants, bulging biceps accentuated by tight polo shirts, the short, watery-eyed, mustachioed *guajiros,* worm-eaten, their wives bloated from childbirth, big-hipped, looking sixty at twenty-five, formed the parade, pushing slowly, gawking, some walking, children running in circles, buzzing, playing with goats dropping round marbles, black, from an assembly line.

The Cadillacs weaved up the roadway, watched by the laughing townspeople. Inside the cars, the heads stared straight, oblivious to the children shouting "*Mira! ¿Te parece al Cristo? Es demasiado blanco.*"

The generals stood erect, an effort, waiting for *El Presidente* to arrive. The band fidgeted, knees slightly bent, uncomfortable in the sticky December air. The Cuban generals wished the West Point dignitaries Merry Christmas, exchanging jokes, ignoring the fifty-foot Lord.

Even after the assemblage was complete the always-present nervous children, barefooted, parasite-infested, pushing, picking noses, stirred around the edges of the crowd. The President arrived, encircled with security; faces smiled; his dark-skinned wife trying not to stare and admire the mulatto features on the white statue.

The band played the Mozart-inspired national anthem, the Archbishop blessed the edifice, two generals and a cabinet minister applauded the art work and then the President was introduced. The crowd stirred at the edges: children twitched.

"This statue will stand as an eternal vigil..." The sun disappeared, black clouds drifted, diluting the bright blues of Caribbean sky and sea into dull gray, a watery, untropical gloom. "Here at the entrance of Havana Harbor we shall have a symbol, a fortress that will protect the people..." The soldiers allowed their eyes to glance at the blackness moving towards them from the sea, almost magnetically directed by the mountain of human-shaped marble. The President was shaking the hand of the artist, while others patted him on the back, loud applause now dying off, hollow, echoing. "He has created for the people an eternal vigil against the evil of atheistic communism."

The harbor was electrified, a lightning spotlight, brightening the dreary unloading of tankers, the frantic Malecon traffic; the flash of unexpected terror at the Fun House. All eyes were drawn heavenward, the band playing a march, the director frantically trying to rush the ceremony without leaving out any preplanned parts. Thunder. The red-shirted, red-skirted, low-cut-bloused, watery-eyed children, paled, chilled and dispersed, stumbling down dirt hills, through makeshift clotheslines, avoiding the goats, munching, dropping pellets. The *Bembe* cults, *cha cha* walks, hurrying, scurrying through paths and bushes for shelter before the watery blackness engulfed the exposed. The Cadillacs were well along the curvy descent, soldiers marching along the side, the head of El Cristo now invisible. The artist and some of the dignitaries ran for shelter at the nearby weather station, waving goodbye to *El Presidente* and his *señora*, who returned the wave from inside of his armor-plated Cadillac. Alone, the statue stood, looking through the gloom when the ziggedy flash snaked downward cutting El Cristo's feminine head in half, leaving only a full mouth, shaped into a bizarre grin.

1960

MULTICULTURALISM

I admire the stoic
squatting peasant
waiting
    for the bus
    the rain
    the sun to set
but his
thoughts
                elude
                    my
                        streaking
                                curiousity

January 1993

RHYMED EVOLUTION

(FOR EE & EB)

Where did the pigeon search for his supper
'midst the forest trees of old,
before the man with the bread crumbs was born
and earth — not land to be sold?
Where was the mouse in the hole in the wall,
'fore the house with walls was built?
Lost in the damp hay in a horse's stall;
His mother smotherd'm in guilt.

My view of the past shows nothing but scorn,
for history quite simply is bunk;
Yet, there's a glimmer of memory torn,
buried in some attic trunk.
I have evolved, I conclude with a sigh,
with pigeons, mice and computers;
My forebears saw only birds in the sky,
no one considered commuters.

October 1991

SATURDAY NIGHT

Like an old time
movie dancer the sky
did a split and
night charged in hurling
terrible threats. Imagine my
surprise when hanging violets
spit out flies like
tobacco chewers outside memphis
or talahassee. Nobody figured
a ziggy zaggy lightning
bolt would fry them
on their porch. White
folks sit around and
dress casual on saturday
night. Storm or not.

November 1992

HOMAGE TO AN INNOCENT POET

What would you say now
that time has passed through
your rattling bones?
Now that trenchant rhymes
grow dull with rapping noise
on walkman phones?
Will you go then
you and I
to see how time
has passed you by?
Your words once slid with soot
from reddened, brown, brick chimneys
interred with acid wit of
ant-a-gon-is-tic Sween-ey
in massive floating garbage tombs
where once pure wasteland loomed.
    "Look,"
I want to shout at the dead,
    "wisdomless decades have afflicted rivers,
distressed trees, burdened soil."
    What could you know of urban blight
    as you eased yourself to twilight
lost in ethereal high
an eternal yellow fog and sky
now brown with silicon scum and slime,
horizons pink and black and lime.
The rooms remain, you know,
where women come and go and drink,
speak of money, weight and shrinks,
cross their flirting, skirted knees
and hope to avoid some new disease;
in salons where poets' lines resound
confused in frenzied disco sound
and foxy smiles and violent feet

where no one knows a line of Greek.
Agamemnon fades in silent protest
like weeping trees in Blackest Forest.
    I read you, urbane poet, long since dead,
    re-emerging as naive optimist; instead,
    wars have surpassed understanding;
    science, an industry, notwithstanding
    those who dare to express, in terms absurd
    with elongated nouns and concocted verbs,
    a disdain for all that once meant Hell.
They no longer sleep in cheap hotels,
or converse in idioms buried in sea shells,
like Wednesday's ashes; jet streams obscure the clouds,
green hills of Bavaria have lost their dip and rise,
First ladies at banquets dress in elegant shrouds
'neath cold, dry heavens; enigmatic saffron skies.

November 1985 - June 1993

THE DECLINE OF AMERICA

(TO JACK)

Somewhere a bell tones
to banish furies from
the heart lure of
order wave of lucidity
an airy bath oil
to wash away woes

I grasp for my bell
strain for childhood rattles
settle for a ring
a buzz alarm of phones
promising lying assuring perpetuity

Old orgies banished with new plagues
whiskey's nectar converted
to pressure on bladder
a five-year-old still clutches the sun
rejects his accomplishments

Wisdom-scorned love diluted
the campanile peals
intones ancient sensibility
modern chaos banal youth
deaf to the sweet chime

An urge to spit strike smite
at mourning papers
Unconvinced by melodies
droners unheard dismissed
no pausing to heed the fortune teller

February 1987

THE LIVING NEED A POEM

The Cold War is over
why aren't we having fun
I have destroyed my internal Timex
kicked an innocent dog
stiffed four ratty beggars
my team has triumphed over
the incarnation of wickedness
I etch acrid sarcasm
on a child's mind
can I pull a poem from shrapnel
fashion words of beauty
from shrill shrieks of falling bombs
submerge the laments of those
with investments
in times of need
the living need a poem

1991

PART 2
KISSINGER AT THE PRADO

KISSINGER AT THE PRADO

It starts with the breaking of my back tooth;
In seconds, I go into minor shock,
I whine,
Guernica in my molars.
"How will I chew?" I ask Goya's hag.
"Vot duss it represent?" a basso profundo queries.
175 years of silent screaming unheard;
A thick Viennese way with words
cuts through lithping Madrileño walla,
"Can similar verks be bought?"

Christ leaks dried blood on ancient icons;
Saints' heads on platters fill rooms;
Guides trained implore the tourists
to understand what they see —
and later buy the prints.
What do they know of the whistling
through the hole of my tooth?

Hunters in search of teeth
acquire symbolic meaning;
My tongue retraces spaces
that once contained integrity;
A Japanese woman giggles,
poses 'neath scheming beggars
Flash!
"For Velazquez vot do you pay?"

A humble peasant lies in comrades' arms;
Frantic German shoppers flip through prints
glancing at Strobl, fixing on Goya:
"Vot does it signify?" booms the voice of authority.
"Is it five in the afternoon?" I want to inquire.

I find a taberna for my tooth,
stake a place at the bar;
Dieting yuppies tap feet
to disco beat;
Ignore me and
baby eel tapas,
sip Stoli, forget vino tinto,
flamenco, Moors, sorrow.

On boulevard Gran Via
swollen hands piden limosnas;
Subjects of painters, poets'
souls imprinted on canvas,
backdrops for tourist photos.

The white-shirted man
raising worker's arms;
The French musketeers aim;
Ernest's bell silent;
Bag ladies extracting tolls;
My broken tooth distracts me;
Sex shops, video games intimidate;
Franco, the internacionalistas,
brave torreros, comrades
in solemn tombs beseech:
"Did we die for this?"
Outside, Manolete swerves deftly
to miss the midday traffic.

December 1989

NORBERT REST IN PEACE

Death tried to enter your nose
you snorted, whisked him away
for day after day after day
to watch the beatings on the screen
you worried about figures called Jews
brutes with clubs making TV news
then rabbi-pushing relatives intrude
perhaps maybe ten years were shaved
perhaps maybe you didn't misbehave

"It doesn't amount to a hill of beans"
you meant nazis and plastics
Vienna school days and crisp wafers
mixing marriage and army-childhood scenes
green bouncing balls, tango, waltz
pulled muscles in the side and long walks
intense morphine cloud pastry dreams
guilt and justice clash at Auschwitz and Gaza
in steamy Central America and Santa Cruz

I'm not afraid to die, you said
the doctors fucked up, the x rays,
the scans, the pills, the tests
you push your fragile body up in bed
bones strain, rattle, yellowed skin stretches
a wipe of nose a sneer at death
I still read everything you said
your eyes fight open, to let in light
you want facts, news, a story of girls
you drifted, coma face drawn with vicious flu
I told you in sleep about just men
and why it's hard to love a state
and you heard or you didn't, I hope you knew
that the daughter will not suffer

or the granddaughter for sins of the father
"Am I," you said, "an anti-semitic Jew
a self-hater at the end, a failure?"
an exercise to prove skepticism's power?

No, I assure face twitching
from the gnawing inside.
No, I assure the sleeping form:
Norbert Rest in Peace

Norbert Frosch was a friend who died before I could accumulate money for him to invest for me, so I could feel financially secure.

1988

WHERE IS FDR?

I miss the confident voice,
overstuffed chair;
Sounds of sewing needles,
radio crackle;
Assurance of the president,
the presiding father
in an apartment
without a fireside;
Mother's overdone roasts
fill my plate;
Kindle ceremonial arguments
about her motives;
At the roof's edge
the tar bubbles froze;
A gritty sparrow dove
for a dirty crust of rye;
A sadistic boy
tossed a mangy cat down
below where wind-blown
Bungalow Bar wrappers
danced in dusty street patterns
with dried pigeon droppings.

Rabbis with dingy beards
spoke no English,
kicked dogs,
owned blocks of buildings,
crouched against walls
when mysterious nuns
paraded by with
ominous, dark habits,
confining caps;
Grandma cupped her flabby hand
over my untutored eyes

muttering guttural Yiddish,
ancient purifying phrases
to counter evil eye,
evil eye, don't look;
I imagined milky drippings
from bulging pupils
emitting invisible rays;
Permanent curses
crawl inside my nostrils,
worm their way among
coils of cerebral spirits.

Outside sterile cathedrals,
I nod to legions of pesty poor,
foolish enough to avoid
balmy southern weather;
Sidewalk toll booths'
shaking, outstretched hands
inciting me to leap
into pits of grief;
Perpetual pallor glowing
with lascivious retribution
from a million evil eyes;
I wait for the president;
My father, trying
to unshroud what I did
to suspend them from providence;
Fathom what transgression
I committed to banish them
to icy battlefields,
drowning in the mud of eternity,
freezing in snows of amnesia.

February 1993

FOR SHIRLEY
(AFTER SHE DIED)

Tenebrous clouds suspended,
judges' robes threatening to flick dandruff
on fearful and unsuspecting parishioners.
Mouths in a million fast food oases
surround gooey Danish and spar with plastic
coffee holders, trying not to scald,
to unstick the soggy dough from gums,
bottoms from chairs, tears from eyes.

Another day,
another car to buy,
nothing's ever finished,
I decide,
no chore quite completed,
no loose end tied
in boy scout knot.
Omega is just a letter,
I conclude,
book closed,
telephone unhooked,
shade drawn,
so mourning clouds cannot intrude
the door secure,
I discover.

Dylan intoned, "Deep with the first dead,"
at White Horse Tavern, NY, NY,
trolled about dark veins of the mother,
as if her voice would always ring
in boozy bars with pot-bellied men;
afterwards, on the answering machine
the light chimes,
the lilt that paced her duty-bound nature,

the effort in her voice, straining
to conduct the orchestra in temperate range.

Hard to goad her into mischief,
a gambler without premonition;
her twinkles flickered pious delights,
Mr. Death himself,
who strikes the fearful,
restrained by her sober valiance.

I could accuse Justice of premature robbery,
or ask Pythagoras to find a proper animal's soul
to slip by night into a still orifice
'ere flames forever scorch the seed of whimsy.

February 1991

She insisted that he stop, and he did. "Real cowboys," she said. He muttered that they would dirty the car upholstery and their fleas would bite the baby, but she had already scooped the infant's paraphernalia off the back seat, twisting her body, baring part of an engorged nursing breast. The two young men ducked their heads climbing in. He gunned the motor before they had closed the door, causing the last one to stumble. He wrinkled his nose; his wife laughed, eyes sparkling with excitement.

"Where you guys headed?" he tried to approximate a western drawl.

"Cheyenne."

"We can only take you part of the way."

They nodded, he saw through the rear view mirror.

The summer wind blew away their smell of cow and horse and all the stuff one connects with animals, sweat and bathlessness. His wife twisted to look at them, and he could feel her glowing. She smiled at them reassuringly, while the baby slept in her arms.

"Careful you don't wake the kid," he said without turning his eyes from the road.

"Are you really cowboys?"

"Yes'm," said the taller one.

"What exactly do you do?"

"Jes work a lil, you know, nothin much," the taller one continued.

"We goin to a rodeo in Cheyenne," said the short one.

"Oh, but don't you work on a ranch and whadayacallit..." she asked.

"Punch cows," he said without turning, with sarcasm that only she caught. The baby moaned from the discomfort of its position.

"Sometime, when there's work," said the short one.

The wind noise now prevailed. He turned on the radio, and found nothing but country music. He looked back at their stoic faces, not indicating their disappointment when he turned the radio off. About twenty years old, he calculated from the fuzzy growth on their faces. The blue jeans and jackets, the broken-in cowboy hats — they could have come from central casting. One pulled a Camel from a rumpled pack and offered. The road sign said 28 miles to Cheyenne, and he felt that he could not endure another half an hour. Their presence was torture to him.

"Where do you live?" his wife asked.

"Wyoming," they both said.

"Do you work most of the year?"

"Sometime," said the tall one.

"We'll be goin to work for the oil and coal company," said the shorter one. "Soon's they start up round here."

"It'll pay good," said the tall one.

"Well," he said, "lots of luck. We're going to stop and eat and rest and change the baby and figure out if we want to get to Cheyenne." He pulled into the truck stop.

"Yes," added his wife, "good luck at the rodeo."

They waved as they walked toward the highway. She watched their firm, bowed, muscled legs. He opened the trunk of the car, took out a whisk broom and began to sweep the back seat.

"They didn't seem like I thought cowboys would be," she said.

"And how are cowboys supposed to be?"

"I don't know. They were so quiet and young."

"And dirty," he added.

"Yes," she said, a little wistfully, still looking at them walking.

"And stupid," he said. His hands shook with rage as he took the baby from her. In the restaurant he again tried to simulate a western accent. The waitress smiled at the baby.

In the booths sat young men with stetsons, jeans and dirty cowboy boots. Their trucks were parked outside. She looked at them; some were staring at her. Her glow faded. It had been a disappointment.

1960

MY DAD WAS NOT HAMLET

Dread?

The infinite regret of words unsaid,
at death's bed and for decades before;
the educated lack of grace,
the unpardonable delinquency of pride,
unadorned and unctuous; a thousand moral cowlicks
defying the rabbis' pleas to forgive.

Imagination?

Did I ever think of my father as Prince of Denmark?
clad in despair, unable to rise above his pajamas
in the mid afternoon?
He did not play a flute nor dispatch
his enemies to watery graves,
nor postpone his solemn duties.

Revenge?

To organize armies against the grandchildren
of the Don Cossacks,
fiery battalions to vanquish Polish hordes?
Did treachery lurk behind my mother's arras?
Plots by foolish uncles to filch his good name?
The vices of the Kiev ghetto in Miami.

Grievances?

If my eyes could have watched his,
spiraling into untranslated dark depths,
could I understand the shame of impotence
in the face of business contracts with cousins?

Clutch the slights and slaps offered
as insults to long-dead relations?

Electricity?

Why did I not grasp his muted appeals?
And make of them a three-act play,
in which, I could forgive my mother her sin,
the inculcation in her son of ignoble weakness;
and let his scattered remains fall,
uncorrupt and unconstrained in final sleep?

May 1990

ME AND MY FLAG

Wrinkled hankies belonging to giants
hang limp, embracing flag poles;
My eye moistens, blood pumps
in accelerated spurts.
No cumulus cloud causes visceral vibrations;
no fragrant rose inspires unusual ardor.
Bodies tense around me,
trumpets empty their excited glands;
rows of men forge elbows into khaki weather vanes,
distort postures,
direct focus.
Machine-dyed patterns,
overwhelming the overhead flying falcon,
subsuming the burrowing gopher,
out-weep the ancient willow;
wind whistles, ambience for agitated perorators.

I drift toward primitive rhythms,
sing internal sonatas in minor keys
of Dead Seas,
broken childhood covenants made with
imaginary partners in dusty western games
on dirty dog doo lots of rubble.
My inert furry pets, whom I comforted
through a millennium of eroding innocence,
restrain my urge to blame,
to transfer the wonderful attributes of evil
to unknown enemies far away;
toys and cars console my grief;
unworthy tears, fallen for a life time
of broken objects,
dry in dusty gusts,
form blueprints of abstract meaning,

I return to sinuous sensations,
pulsating strength drawn from brass and drum;
discipline of bodies in aerobic striding,
boots, bouncing in unison
on pavement,
echoing like jungle beats,
the message to obedient citizen-soldiers,
blended by modern alchemy into a team,
honoring the multi-colored bandana's
noblest flutters,
beyond my trivial respirations.
Who could oppose the cementing vigor,
the marshalled beauty of invulnerable appearance?

My ancient rabbi shrugs,
his stooped shoulders do not rise
to the occasion of unbroken faith;
a smug sneer etched on wrinkled jaw
responds to stirring words by mocking
the very sky itself, God's witness
to the transcendent quality of the event.
No frightened deer stops to drink in nearby stream,
no baby crawls where marching men have tromped.
The formations themselves purge the despair
of flagging hearts,
casualties of inadequate love,
memorizers of lamentations and celebrations.
I feel prepared to meet my foes,
I care not for the gray beneath the sun;
no symbols from Heaven can submerge
the power of pennants unfurled,
foreground for mighty mountains.
I buy a plastic miniature.
Inside the clamorous stadium
I push through throngs,
the disciples who share

the noises of deep affection.
I sing, I salute, secure in identity,
participating in events of my time.

March 1990

LOVE

STAGE 1

A gentle wind fluttered
at the nape of my neck;
a quiet green lake
rippled on a mountain
trail in subdued autumn;
a strand of straw
blew across a yellow
meadow, a fragile pine
branch prepared to receive
the first snow flurry.
Inside, a bead of sweat
glistened, a dew drop
poised above your mouth,
a tempting tulip petal
emitting peppermint tea
with your humming a
glowing log snapped
its contemptuous message
while amber stones glistened
in moonlight. From your
velvet skin wafted attar
of gardenias; a squirrel
dissolved into desert nymphs
signing autographs in silken sands.

STAGE 2

Have I smothered your landscape?
Discolored your grandma's quilt?
Clogged your sturdy arteries
with malodorous chicken soup,
recipes of frightened migrants?

Have I infiltrated your dreams
with inclement images,
netherworlds unexplored by pioneers
to drain your heavy sleep
with unnatural syringes of compulsion?
Have I cracked your delicate aura
with effluvia of alien suffering?
Invaded your spontaneity
with obligations of incongruous Deities,
fears of agonized retribution?

Have I brought Golem and Dybbuks
to untune the upright piano?
Inundated your forests
with pernicious gases from dim layers
where intricate worms hide in recess?

STAGE 3

Can I take my passion with
you from a common spring?
Place my storm inside
your untroubled breast?
Leave the drafty coffin
of irritable ancestors?
Can I sustain my war inside
the temptation of love?
Will my delight in your flesh
loosen the ropes of torment?
Will my phlegmatic demons
sear your smooth skin?
I awake at night to
find them hiding in
familiar corners of
the murky swamps of
memory.

Will you hear my
midnight cries
and banish the
fiends who disturb
our peace?

1984

PART 3
ANXIETY IN THE REDWOODS

NATURE AND ME

The sight of the bee fills me with fear
Who belongs and who does not?
I slay ants with almost no pang of conscience
Other invaders suffer equal fate
How dare they threaten me?

Dangerous forms of life in all sizes
Man-eating flowers, undersea clams
Loom like voracious carnivores
I am not Tarzan, I meekly confess
Neither fearless hunter nor scuba diver

A ferocious squirrel crosses my path
"How cute" says the little girl
Unaware of rabies and pestilence
I would have squashed the black bird
That flew by mistake into my kitchen

The calmest sea contains images
Blood rituals, sharks that bite at night
The benign-looking jellyfish best had in salad
I am not easily tricked by so-called Nature
A cunning, tempting, seductive abstraction

I stand with my sword unsheathed against the world
A cement-bound ingratiating soldier
I take orders from my dead ancestors
Who distance themselves from sentimentality
I defy alien jungles, murderous mountains

I like the smell of freshly-sliced flowers
Does the butcher care about the slaughter of cows?
Does the baker weep over the massacre of wheat?
I remain as far from God as he from Me
I refuse to pray just to postpone my banishment

1986

CARIBBEAN CRUISE

No December chill bites my soul
nor winter shadows dog my trail;
Dubious obligations goad me aboard.
Like Ishmael I inhale the sour, salt breeze;
Like Ahab, I hide in my cabin to let
rancid memories drive my voyage.
Through a porthole I search the horizon
for the spout of great whales.

The Nordic Empress plowed through endless rows of
waves,
'neath her decks no stokers work, yet her engines blazed.
I watched in vain for copper suns to scorch a bloody sky,
I sipped an icy pina drink; the fish I ate was fried.

I saw no whales nor floating bergs of sharpened ice,
no graceful porpoise swam 'side the speeding ship;
Nor albatross o'er the polished decks, but
blackjack dealers stacked their clacking chips.

It's me and the sea,
no lifeguards or mermaids,
no kind keeper of the Eddystone light,
me and seaweed,
styrofoam cups,
Jaws and riptides.
Coney Island
to Miami Beach.
Oh, yeah! Life at sea,
you and me,
and
the dramamine.

January 1991

BRIEF ANXIETY IN THE REDWOODS

The wary slum-dweller
s
t
e
p
s
on pine carpet
Eyes shift
ing
to spy
an ambush set by rattlers.
Ears tuned
for signals of
charging wild boar.
Nostrils flared
to catch
scents of passing bears.

Watchful for lyme ticks
alert for poison oak
the cautious urbanite undertakes adventure.
He may confront
man-eating eagles,
poisonous moths and toads
spewing warty juice.

The Brooklynite Unarmed
with Natty Bumppo's poise and skills
hears his heart punch
the chest wall.
Nature's drapes block the cancerous sun rays.
Just ahead
the highway promises discreet safety.

1985

NATURAL QUESTIONS

"You never looked better,"
I flattered a squirrel,
in a passably philosophical tone.

"How do you manage your mal de mer,"
I queried an indulgent possum,
"in the wet, heavy air of a swamp?"

I ponder the weary autumn grass:
Would it begrudge us growth
if we refused the ritual rake?

"Would summer postpone its inevitable fall,"
I propose to a serious dog.
"Would bees buzz our salads in March?"

"Do pumpkins spray October hues,"
I ask of a pumpkin patch,
"to burn the hennaed wind?"

"How do your colors radiate mirth,"
ask my delighted eyes,
"and match your hair to a squash?"

"Must you fidget as Halloween nears,"
I ask of a frightened boy,
"and nettle my restless sleep?"

October 1991

DOMESTICATED METAMORPHOSES

You dress a turkey
    put on a little make up
    POOF you've got a peacock
Or didn't ya notice the feet
    the palsied head
    fancy clothes don't boost appetites
                                        ya know

You stripe a big tom
    a mean old alley cat
    WOW this mini tiger can scare you
Follow the fee-line
    murderous speed of a claw
    blinding a barking, slow-witted dog
                                        uh huh

You unleash a cactus
    remove fat brown slugs
    YUK hanging on wing bottoms
You don't have to major
    in aviary aerodynamics
    to figure that prickly zeppelin
                                        oh boy

Imagine rice moving
    maggots wiggle on plates
    GOD you're drunk or tripping
You see grains crawl
    slither on salad
    till ya fork em and eat em
                                        ya know

1993

APRIL FOOLS

Do I detect a tear dropping
from the bud on the branch
on the trunk of the tree?
Misplaced sylvan emotion
mourning winter's passing;
Or is it acid, April rain
burning the eager grass?

1987

THE NATURE OF A WAITRESS

A cross
s
w s
i g
n
amidst

e a
l a v g (it's a sin to look?)
c e
when she b
e
n
d
s to serve
a beer to
a man who
has neither
parched throat
nor desires
to sip brew
any more than a w e a r y lioness
ponders a 3 mile j$_{o}$g in the jungle

Crooked teeth flash amidst
a
s e
m l
i
her jaw will throb b b again
at the end
of the day
the arbit-
rary hour

of desires
of drinking
no more natural than a c a
canary
g e d
singing for simple pleasures.

March 1993

NEW ENGLAND AUTUMN

Frosty woods hide secrets of clever poets
frigid rivers etch design on flat pebbles
Increase Mather's sermon whistles through
the birches "Evil is pleasure"
a sturdy pumpkin beams All Saints' smile
stoic before the gnawing ants inside
in the house beds unmade quilt askew
yearnings unsatisfied warmth of breast
and wine miles away prayers muted by
ghostly icy wind messages pitched
to blow by organ pipes o'er frigid fields.

The wagon rickety-racks over cobblestones
trampling chips of Puritan relics
wet and slithering wiggleworms cover
tangled cracks in the roadway over
tunnels to rotted chasms of memories
twisting tubes of decayed cocoons
passages to layers of sin cavities rife
with misers' money burning without flame
in obscure Salem woods and arbors
Jonathan Edwards' warning ripples
through the thistles "Pleasure is our nature."

The symmetrical flight of ducks and geese
the slow deterioration of the birch bark
the thinning of hair on Father's head
the paling of summer hues on skins the
family prepares for the Autumn drift
Mother pulls sweaters from drawers to meet
the fall of leaves the muting of frogs
Devil's colors secure their pernicious hold
have their way with the ends of the branch
careful dogs inter their precious bones
"A beacon in the Wilderness," said Winthrop.

November 1987

IN THE EVERGLADES

Watch!
The striped butterfly bounces,
a nonchalant, novice pilot
negotiates invisible landing strips;
A purposeful, floating M. Hulot
eluding the web stretched across
the treacherous manzanillo where
the serious arachnid prevails,
weighted with obligations on every leg
ignoring the frivolous springtime flitter.

I dare not dangle my toe in the clear gray pond
nor boldly step into oceans of grass beyond
I breathe the serenity of uncountable creatures
agitated with missions that drive their natures

Watch!
The snowy egrets ever alert
for a slithering fish,
unconcerned with ticklish, chocolate logs
protruding above the glass surface
of maturing water lapping the bank;
Mangroves drop their branches
in phallic staves, sucking
murky juice from the shifting floor
where creatures crawl in sagacious slime.

I stare at a viper on a mahogony tree
as shrill finches intone at the danger they see
along the branch writhing, a deep, dangerous brown
it slides ever upward, a lot safer than down.

Moist!
I emerge from the evening shower

my sun-stung flesh medium rare
lightly baked, deftly punctured;
Persistent mosquito drilling
her hole to extract my nectar
while I untutored examined the nature
of morning glories wrapping
thoughtless vines in late afternoon
around the acned trunk of the buttonwood.

In summer dry pines suffer parchment with fires
I wail in silence against deviant desires
Herr Himmler's camera clicks once at the crows,
Frau Himmler's binoculars rise to her nose.

Watch!
I challenge the onset of tranquility,
in desperation grasp myself in a headlock
a tenacious night wrestler
knowing dawn will liberate me
from the chokeholds of wise men;
I imagine consequences derived
from shortcake cravings, extinction of snakes
lust for spicy pizzas at midnight.

Follow the ibis at dawn in ethereal flight
thin lines on the sun in soft morning light
the pelican smashing the surface for prey
ten thousands of years dissolve in its spray

March 1993

PART FOUR
THE AGE OF REVOULUTION — AND PAIN

VOLCANO

The volcanic lake sparkled. The eleven o'clock sun blistered the skin on our bodies but made the lake look clearer. The volcano puffed in the background. We passed a group of men swimming some 50 feet from shore and we made beach camp far away enough so that we could only hear them when they raised their voices—which they did with more frequency as the morning merged into afternoon.

Antonio had begun drinking the night before, beer at dinner, the bottle of Jack Daniels I had bought at the duty-free store at the airport, more beer for breakfast. He wasn't totally obnoxious yet, but I felt he could easily get there. The rest of us went swimming. Antonio sipped beer on the lake shore. He had insisted we stop and buy some. It had been too long, he told us, since he had freed himself from his bureaucratic behavior.

"I want to go back to the north and fight again. I want to clean them up," he proclaimed, with a bottle of Toña in his hand. The rest of us swam, and the warm and cold currents from the volcanic craters shot us in the limbs like stimulants. Ricardo's mangled foot felt better in the water, Nancy told me. But his two remaining toes appeared to be embedded in a slab of raw meat.

I had watched him limp from the spot where he parked his vintage Cutlass. He tried to walk naturally, and had I not been studying his gait I would not have noticed. The shrapnel could not be extracted, the doctors had told him.

Maria Rosa had carefully picked up the string bag of fresh fruit and followed her cousin. Ricardo's .45 showed beneath the flapping shirt tail as he walked on the rock and dirt path past the lakeside village, which consisted of a few houses and a bar-restaurant-grocery store with a juke box. It showed no sign of war. Animals grazed lazily. The air seemed to hang. Yet we were not far from Managua's sprawling clusters of dwellings, interspersed with fields of weeds where houses had been before the earthquake, from the bombed homes and factories, the stucco houses with bullet and shell dents, like pockmarks on the houses' faces, the ruins, rusting, ivy-covered, rotting, the Nicaragua that most visitors saw. War monuments on the highway and on the streets of Masaya needed no explanation. Acrylic signs along the roadways demanded that the illiterate majority eat, drink, buy some expensive product.

The majority ignored the signs. They possessed little money with which to accommodate the imperative messages. On the highway, those with whiter faces and newer clothes drove most of the vehicles, ate at the roadside restaurants, noticed the brightly-colored advertisements designed and placed by members of their family, clan, tribe, class. The Nicaraguan bourgeoisie was enjoying itself, but nevertheless felt insecure. They did not have the weapons at their disposal to insure the future satisfaction of their consuming urges.

Ricardo and Nancy sunned themselves, occasionally touching hands. Antonio sipped the last of his beer. I felt hot, not like sun-bathing with the younger people. I dressed and walked to the restaurant with my notebook. Maria Rosa remained in the shade, guarding our things and Ricardo's .45.

I ordered a flor de caña rum, opened my notebook and started to write notes about my impressions of the road to Masaya. Women with Indian faces sold but did not hawk the plastics and the gadgets alongside of the artisan-crafted blouses and leather goods. Few buyers. Loud radio. My writing is interrupted by the blaring juke box.

I look around annoyed. A large man has inserted coins and is making multiple selections. "Beer," he shouts at the young boy who serves the drinks. Other men walk into the arbor-covered patio. The lake sparkles between the trees in front of me. An almost imperceptible shiver catches me unaware. The blaring static flow of words about love and lost love mixes with orders for beer, lusty guffaws and hearty laughter. The men are mostly in their late 20s and early 30s. Some ten are now gathered and slurping beer rapidly. They have military postures and some have the U.S. Marine-style haircut.

Dogs and pigs prowl behind the tables as if humbly acknowledging that anyone can throw them anything and they'll eat it. Ricardo and Nancy begin walking down the narrow dirt path toward the restaurant. The sun has disappeared behind a cloud. The small boy who serves the beer plants a vicious kick in the ribs of one of the dogs. The dog yips and flees. The pigs get the hint, but not before one gets a kick in the snout from the kid. The juke box blares a weeping song featuring a tinny accordion. The men dance with each other. A chicken struts around the rear edge of the tables, its head not quite twitching in tempo with the accordion.

Ricardo and Nancy arrive with Maria Rosa and the possessions. Antonio trails behind. The sun has tired them, warmed them. They are hungry and thirsty. Except for Antonio, who looks pale, almost green. The volcano burps a little smoke; a cloud rims its tip like a halo. Coconuts and papayas hang from the foreground trees, and flies and other insects dot the air. The small winged creatures seem to thrive and grow larger in the warm climates.

I steal another look at the men, husky, rough. A beer-bellied man shouts at his mates in a command voice. Some of his partners have grown beards. They dance awkwardly with each other, making theater out of their impending drunkenness, sometimes turning dancing into wrestling. They appear not to notice our presence.

I pretend nothing is wrong. Nancy and Maria Rosa move toward the ladies' room. Ricardo and I remain at the table. Antonio walks slowly down the path. Ricardo is quiet, lets his glasses slip partway down his nose. He looks like a student. Three years ago he was. Antonio arrives and moves toward the bathrooms, grunting as he sees the dancing, drinking men.

"You think they're ex-*guardia*?" I ask Ricardo.

"They look like ex-*guardia*," he answers.

The beer-bellied man makes a short, incomprehensible speech. The juke box noise drowns out part of his words. The men are moaning, mourning, laughing, punching each other's arms, reminiscing. There is a group leader: a younger, better-dressed man, without the military look and posture. He keeps ordering the drinks. He notices us, purses his lips into a polite smile. Ricardo looks straight ahead, a slight facial twitch the only sign of emotion he shows.

Nancy and Maria Rosa return, dressed, showered. "Someone's in the men's room puking his guts out," Nancy comments.

"Antonio," says Ricardo.

"It's disgusting to get drunk," Nancy sneers. Maria Rosa looks straight ahead.

"He must have needed to do it or he wouldn't have done it," Ricardo says without intonation in his voice. "Let's move tables," he adds. He rises, negotiates the move with a nervous man who apparently supervises the boy, and we move our drinks and napkins to the table farthest from the cavorting men. The men still pretend not to notice our presence. Ricardo does not look at them. But his hand moves behind him, he feels for his weapon, making certain the shirt tail is loose.

Antonio returns. "No more drinks," he says to the boy. Ricardo and I smile. "Shit, man," Antonio says, shaking his head, "I forgot how to drink. Man I gotta get north again. I can't stand life at the goddamn desk anymore. I needed get high so bad."

Nancy looks away at the lake. No one is swimming. We order hot food. I sip flor de caña. Ricardo orders another beer. Nancy and Mana Rosa drink fruit punch. Antonio shakes his head. "I'll wait a while." We all force smiles.

The man with the marine haircut stumbles toward the bar, shouting at the young boy. "Where's the beer?" The older man smiles, assures him that it will soon come. The drunk's eyes flash toward our table.

"Fucking *guardia* man. The revolution is too goddamn generous," Antonio snaps. "Man, if I had my Uzi I'd have a hell of a hard time to keep from just spraying those motherfuckers."

"Yeah," Richardo drawls, "we'll probably have to do it sooner or later. Why not now?" Three years ago, when he dropped out of Stanford University in his senior year, he was an *A*-student in political science.

"Maybe they're not *gaudia*," Nancy says to Ricardo. "How can you be so sure?"

Ricardo replies slowly, "One's still wearing the cap Somoza handed out to his pack." Nancy holds Ricardo's hand under the table.

We leave after paying. The older man no longer looks concerned. "The people watch them," Ricardo tells me reassuringly. "The *guardia* can't do much shit here. Some of them will go to Honduras, link up with the rest of the gang and then stage raids on the north."

"Yeah," Antonio adds. "Fuck 'em, right Ricardo? Shit. I'd rather be back in the mountains than sitting at my goddamn desk."

We trudge down the dirt road with all our gear to where Ricardo has left the Oldsmobile. We are tired. It has a flat. Ricardo opens the trunk. No spare. No jack or tools either. It is hot and dry. The buzz of insects seems to increase in volume.

Several cars pass. Nancy and Maria Rosa stop each one,

asking if they have a spare tire to sell or lend. None fit the Cutlass. Finally, Ricardo asks a villager if anyone in town might have a pump. He goes down the road in search of a man who might have one. We wait by the side of the car, receiving sympathetic looks from the passers-by. No Cutlass-size car arrives. Ricardo returns with a bicycle pump. We take turns pumping. Flies and gnats pick away at our exposed skin.

A radio nearby replays a speech by one of the members of the revolutionary junta. It is interspersed with thunderous applause. Most of the words are inaudible, but *revolución, patria, sacrificio* come through, as does *Patria Libre o Morir, Venceremos,* at the end. We blast enough air into the tire to make a try for the main highway.

The climb up the mountain allows us to look back at the lake as the sun begins its descent behind the volcano. The car in front of ours refuses to allow Ricardo to pass. He honks, curses, accepts his fate until the road widens.

Our faces begin to show the first signs of redness. The discomfort of the return trip begins to edge toward our consciousness, the anxiety of the leaking tire, the frustration, the men at the restaurant. We listen to music, Latin rock.

Ricardo reaches the top, makes the turn toward the highway to Masaya, and the sound of a flapping tire, unmistakably a dead tire, overvolumes the engine and radio sounds. Ricardo pulls over at a juncture. Villagers pass by in silent groups. It is the Day of the Dead, Maria Rosa explains, and the villagers are going to and from the cemetery.

A large van chugs by. The dancing men with military postures sit inside it, some sleeping, others almost sleeping. One sees us, grins with pleasure at our predicament. "Fuck you," Antonio mutters. "If I had my Uzi..."

"Man, why don't you get armed while you're here?" Ricardo retorts angrily. "You shouldn't walk without an arm. Look at all those fuckers around. You never know when one of the bastards who was shooting at you in the north will see you and pop you."

Ricardo flags down a new jeep, and the couple inside reluctantly agree to give him a ride to Masaya. Nancy complains that he is stupid to go without taking the tire with him. The jeep's driver becomes irritated. "Take the tire with you," Nancy shouts. "Then you can get it fixed and come back."

"I don't need it," Ricardo maintains. "We don't have a jack to remove it."

"Make up your mind," the driver adds. Ricardo leaves with them. Nancy pouts and complains for a few minutes, then settles down and holds Maria Rosa's hand.

I tell them that the ex-*guardia* were celebrating or mourning the death of Somoza. Nancy scoffs at the idea. Drunks wander by and stare at the flat tire, weave toward and then away from us. The sun drops rapidly. Late-afternoon flies and gnats begin their return to the unknown places whence they came. A delicious cool descends, and Nancy takes the initiative and begins stopping cars, asking if she can borrow their jack. She speaks Spanish like a Nicaraguan. A late-model Chevy stops. The back seat is filled with children, and a woman and a baby sit in front. The man jumps out of the car and opens his trunk. Two drunks pause and discuss the predicament. "*Compa*," says one, "what are they doing?" The man hauls out a tire and then a jack.

I get up to help and discover as I grab the tire that it has been recently painted black. I drop it and grab the jack. It is also sticky with fresh black paint. The man shrugs. No explanation.

We succeed in placing the sticky jack under the front bumper, using the Chevy's headlights to illuminate the scene. "How many goddamn dead are there in this village?" Antonio remarks, as the flow up and down the cemetery hill continues. "They killed more than 50,000," he answers his own question. The car perilously raised on the jack, sways. The man eases Antonio and me aside and removes the tire. But despite the apparent agreement in size between his tire and the Cutlass', something doesn't work; something is warped. We can't fit his spare onto the wheel.

The man's trousers are now covered with black paint, and the children inside the car have caught late-afternoon crabbiness and spread it through the back seat of the car. The man looks at his paint-covered hands, his freshly-laundered pants with fresh black stains and shouts "Shut up!" at the children. His wife's Indian face remains impassive, as does Maria Rosa's. Nancy says "Shit." Antonio accepts the Chevy driver's offer to go to Masaya to repair the tire. "Watch for Ricardo," Nancy shouts. They leave with the flat in their trunk.

Ricardo returns meanwhile in a taxicab. "Wait." he orders the cab driver. He has put 500 cordobas down as a way to keep the one tire repair store in Masaya open. "Find Antonio," Nancy instructs. "He'll be looking for the tire repair store, and if there is only one open you'll find him. He's with a man and a large family in a Chevy." Ricardo jumps back into the cab. The driver is laughing. We are smiling.

Thirst comes with darkness. Maria Rosa goes into the nearest farmhouse. Dogs bark angrily. She re-emerges with a jug of water. I drink even though I fear it will cause me ruin later.

We sit by the roadside and watch the last of the villagers return from the cemetery. Noise abates rapidly and only the insects and birds can be heard. Then the distant sound of music. A party is starting in one of the villages.

Maria Rosa describes a battle in her village. "The *guardias* came and took this boy from his house. They said he was a guerrilla. I don't know. They shot him in the arms, then the legs, laughing, you know. Then one shot him in the head and called his mother. That's how they are, you know."

I think of Nancy's tour of Managua. She showed me the new supermarkets that Somoza built with the earthquake relief money. On the tour Antonio had told me the story of how Ricardo almost lost his foot kicking the grenade. "Guts, man. Ricardo has guts. He kicked that motherfucker and saved the rest of us."

"Yeah," Nancy had added, "and now look at his foot."

Antonio had smiled. "Your niece talks like a cynic, but she's more revolutionary than I am. She's disciplined."

"Do you like it better in Managua than in the village?" I ask Maria Rosa.

"Yes, there's no place to study in the village."

Antonio and Ricardo return in the Chevy with the repaired tire. They change it with the help of the man. Ricardo offers the man money.

"No, no," he says. "I don't take money for helping." I give him the remainder of the flor de caña bottle. His wife offers us some cold and fatty roast pork. We exchange good-byes. Ricardo hurries everyone into the car and starts it. Behind us we hear the Chevy's starter scratching—no turn over. The man had used his headlights again to illuminate the tire-changing. His battery is dead.

"Ricardo," Nancy pleads. Ricardo keeps driving. I turn around. No headlights show behind us. "He has all those kids," she says.

"He's a fucking *Somocista,*" responds Ricardo. "All he talked about was how great things used to be and how he's gonna kick the Sandinistas out," he says. "The revolution is too generous, too goddamned generous."

"He was a nice guy though," Antonio adds. Ricardo says nothing. Nancy tells me about her job, the frustrations and joys of teaching illiterates political education.

"You should be proud of your niece," Antonio says and pats my back.

On the highway Ricardo begins to speed; Nancy whines and he slows down, a little. The traffic in Managua is thin. But Ricardo drives with determination. He has told us that he has an appointment with his commanding officer and he is afraid he might already have missed it.

Antonio begins to snore gently in the back seat. Maria Rosa hums to herself. "The revolution is too generous," Ricardo repeats as we pass billboards painted with slogans of the right-wing party. A few moneychangers still parade near the Intercontinental Hotel as we pass by. "We call them coyotes,'" Ricardo tells me. "We let them change their black-market money. For now. We're very generous."

Their tiny house is hot from the heat of the day. Everyone greets the next-door neighbor seated on the patio. Ricardo's commanding officer hasn't arrived yet. We tell them about the beauty of the lake. The neighbor says it was hot in Managua. "A group of men had a shoot-out near Masaya with the militia," he reports. "We heard it on the radio half an hour ago. Some ten or twelve ex-*guardia*, drunk or something. Some of them were killed; a couple escaped. I don't have all the details."

I feel numbness in my jaw.

"Yeah," says Ricardo. "I'm not surprised. We're too generous, but I don't know what the hell else we can be."

Nancy embraces him, tears escaping from her eye. Maria Rosa brews coffee.

A jeep followed by a car pulls up, and a man with a submachine gun jumps out and greets Ricardo and Antonio. "The *comandante* is here." A small man, maybe two or three years older than Ricardo, crawls out of the car behind the jeep. A bodyguard with an AK-47 crawls out with him. Ricardo and he embrace.

"You look worried," says Maria Rosa to me. "What's the matter?"

Nancy smiles to me. Ricardo brushes his hair, calmly removes his Gallil rifle from the hook in his bedroom. He kisses Nancy. He shakes my hand, reminds me to send him the books I've promised and heads toward the jeep. "I won't forget," I shout, "and take good care of my niece." The jeep pulls away. I don't think he's heard what I've said. But words haven't been too important all day. Inside the house, I think about the word *generosity* and drink my coffee.

1980

JAMAICA FAREWELL

Laughter trickles from ferned gullies
dues, debts, higglers' cries ring, draw
garish patterns, pulsate through Oxford Street
where rastas await the thunder of Joshua's trumpet.

Nectar and timber of Senegal
squeezed twixt palms and water
into bizarre black Sunday suits
mister, missus and please, sir.

"Give them time, give them time!"
Only four centuries have passed;
Mouths protract to torture themselves,
disciplined to unnatural formations.

Like surreal tropical comedy clubs
committees of Parliament sit in procedure,
posing as models of appropriate channels,
rhythms of former, deeper conflicts.

In one day the Babylonians could burn,
the temples, shiny deities crumble,
the painful Nordic inventions of speech
banished in cyclones of pulsating Swahili.

1980

THE ASSASSINATION OF LETELIER AND MOFFITT

On September 21, 1976, agents of the Chilean Intelligence service detonated a bomb underneath Orlando Letelier's car, just as it entered Washington's Sheridan Circle. Letelier was former Chilean Ambassador to the United States (1970-1972) and held several Cabinet posts (1973) under the government of Salvador Allende. After the explosion, Letelier, his legs severed, bled to death. Ronni Moffitt, who was sitting next to him, died shortly after, literally drowning in her own blood from a neck wound. Like Letelier, she also worked at the Institute for Policy Studies, with her husband Michael, who was sitting in the back of the car and miraculously survived the blast with minor wounds.

On the day of the bombing FBI and other police agents vacuumed Sheridan Circle for evidence and questioned people. I was asked by one Special Agent who I thought had done the deed. "DINA," I replied, the acronym for Chile's intelligence service.

"What's her last name?" the agent asked.

Police dogs sniffed their way through IPS while the Institute Directors, Marcus Raskin and Richard Barnet, prepared to hold a press conference to announce that only General Augusto Pinochet, who led the 1973 coup against Allende and subsequently governed Chile as illegitimnate President, could have ordered the kill. Raskin and Barnet would also declare that Isabel Letelier, Orlando's widow, would replace him as a Fellow at the Institute.

The morning after the assassination I awoke and calmly washed, dressed, breakfasted, gathered papers I wanted to take with me to the institute. I walked out to my car and fished the key out of my pocket. When I tried to insert the key into the car door, my hand began to shake, causing me to make tiny scratches in the paint around the key slot. Shock had ended; fear had begun.

I used both hands to get the key into the ignition and closed my eyes and bit my lip as the engine turned over. I imagined sound, flame, smoke, pain, but my Plymouth Fury simply started. The trembling stopped. The involuntary daydreams launched themselves like fast-moving ships inside my head.

By the time I arrived at the IPS building I had conceived a myriad violent deaths for myself, most of them revolving around a car bombing. I also realized that I had to either run away from the whole affair or decide to live with this fear. I could allow my imagination to write horror scripts and invent murderous scenarios, and I could continue to work and function. No conscious decision arose from these thoughts; I simply began to do what had become necessary. Orlando was my friend, my colleague, and my comrade. So was Ronni.

I didn't tell Ralph Stavins (an IPS fellow) my fears; he didn't tell me about his. We just set out with clenched jaws, to push as hard as we could to bring the killers to justice, or at least to expose them.

The majority of people we knew and loved, those who worked with us and lived with us and would have to share whatever consequences our efforts brought, those from afar who cared about justice and who loved Chile, those in power who had liberal views, who knew Orlando, the religious people who wept and said that a great sin had been committed-all these people, as with one voice, told Ralph Stavins and me that we were absolutely crazy to attempt an investigation of these murders. All had different reasons, but all agreed that nothing but more pain and suffering would result from our efforts. Only Isabel Letelier did not object. She wasn't optimistic about our chances for success, but at least she did not disagree with our plans. That was all we needed. We ignored the rest because we did not like their advice. Our reasons were ethical and political. We felt we had to pursue the killers in any and every way that we could.

Reprinted from Assassination on Embassy Row, *by John Dinges and Saul Landau, Pantheon, 1981.*

I DIDN'T KNOW TATI

"Tati" was the nickname of Beatriz Allende, oldest daughter of Chilean President Salvador Allende. She commited suicide. I knew her in Chile and then in Cuba, where she lived and worked as Secretary of *Unidad Popular,* the coalition that governed Chile until it was overthrown in the September 1973 coup, in which her father was killed.

I never saw a raven in her eyes
or black lilies 'round her neck
her voice spoke Fall and Summer chimes;
In her gait the Spring of youth

I could not imagine — my mind's cliche —
the sorrows she dared to feel
nor taste the acid of family wounds
that burned beneath her smile

I never spied a raven on her back
or black lilies in her hair
words said brave and noble deeds;
In her stare the grasp of truth

I did not know — a simple phrase —
of depths she dared to probe
nor divine the slime of torture tales
that boiled within her bowel

I never saw the raven strike her
or black lilies curl 'round her throat
her lips purred blends of confidence;
On her shoulders stood the world

I could not believe — I'd said before —
such gall within her soul
nor fathom depths of human hate
that she had come to know.

October 1977

RODRIGO THE KID

Rodrigo Rojas came to Washington after the 1973 coup, with his mother, a political refugee. He volunteered to do chores at the Institute for Policy Studies, hung around me and others, fascinated with how we were investigating the assassination of Orlando Letelier and Ronni Moffitt. When he became an expert photographer at age nineteen he returned to Chile, part of the Southern Cone of the Western Hemisphere, with his camera and his passion to investigate.

Look what you've done now you little pisher
I want to say to this nine-year-old boy
the gawky adolescent
the pesty kid
whose gangling height gave me a pain in the neck

Don't talk back to your mom I said
a cliche along with papers
to xerox
to collate
while he grew, learned, hung out

At twelve he knew more than I about
copiers, cameras
loneliness, fear
feelings of exile
skepticism, betrayal, and hanging out

Why, why, why he asked
how does it work
what is that for
does this really prove what you say?

I passed him on to others
for apprenticeship in camera stores and dark rooms
to high schools and long corridors
I watched him grow
drop his accent, look after his brother

Another kid in my life
full of kids
pests
growing, making me feel short, old, tired
making me reveal what I was not sure I knew

He took my passport pictures
he didn't like the light
wasn't flattering enough?
Big shot, professional
taking his camera to Chile

Watch your ass I told him
imagine the little pisher
old enough to go to Chile
to take pictures
to worry his mother about new dangers

Imagine, I said, look at the size of him
the way he speaks now
his posture improving
He's really matured
about to find himself

Another shock of recognition
another kid
another friend
another life
ground under the boot in the Cone

Damn that kid I cried
how could he do this to his mother?
To me and others?
Get himself all burned up like that
just like a Jew in a different time

September 1986

DIRGE FOR A DECADE

Ten years, long years, no time at all
A damp, drizzly, sultry morning in my soul
A dry, fidgety feeling of funerals
A dizzy dream of dreary skies
I hurl faceless enemies from lofty palisades
They keep coming, chasing, threatening

A decade has passed, as decades do, with no resolution
Yet we have resolutely made our resolves
To bear indefinitely our friends' infirmities
We have no substitutes for plain and simple faith
Death is the ultimate indignity, the final infirmity
My soul has been insulted; it wants to duel

Ten years ago I invented grievances for murderers
Even attributed motives for their savage spectacles
I heard malicious mountebanks make victims into criminals
Diminishing their graves with spray-painted slogans
Defacing their monuments with cowards' complaints
Achieving pathetic climax by taunting the dead

Do the spirits cry out for justice?
Do the ghosts haunt friends and kin at night?
Oh what formulas for madness, what lures for revenge!
Better that sorrow flow in impersonal churches
Purging passion from the crowded eyes
Soprano voices singing gracias thank you a la vida

My tears have been shed, my anger cooled
Into steady uncreative outrage
A head of state has murdered, aided and abetted
By arch criminals who occupy posts of responsibility
Up here, down there, well-paid by those of comfort
Vile knaves who share sadistic love amongst themselves

Well-paid perjurors orate in international forums,
Organizers of cabals with heady titles bray their hatred,
Triumphantly pronounce patriotic cliches, inane warnings
Formaldehyde creatures convert their greed into elixirs
To prolong their decay, celebrating their stench
In orgies of born-again self-righteousness

Ten years, a lifetime, a snap of the fingers
The miserable and the fortunate voyage of life
He was the noblest Chilean of them all
Gentle and lusty, filled with flaws and hope
She the kindest, sweetest Esther of my tribe
Deprived by modern Ha'man of reproductive rights

Were their natures too noble for this world?
They would not bow before Caesar for his missiles
Nor accept the benefits of complacence
They did not choose their violent death
Naively they rode, secure in their faith
That "the valiant never taste of death but once"

Ten painful years. Is the patient man not mad?
Has tolerance become an unpardonable fault?
As mornings turn murderous gray in Santiago
Have you all not taken some sinful oath
To hold back the just and sweet wrath of revenge
Has God cursed us all with the illusion of gentility?

Alas we know we are not exempt from fear
Only the dead and the noble can make such claims
We expel the fiends of impulse
Force the dark despair from our bosoms
Once every year for in cruel September
We lay siege before our circle of death and life

September 1986

AFTER ELEVEN YEARS

We lay garlands of flowers, a fragrant mourner's tax
burn countless yartzeit candles till they melt into a wax
we imagine the gentle sounds of old Spanish ballads
a young woman played a flute, in the absence of malice

We assumed in privilege we could master our fate
our innocence ended, we mark time, with a date
we learned about the details of mundane killing plans
by creatures descended from Macbeth's ancient clan

We persevere, year by year, more than a decade now
elusive justice dodges blunted arrows from our bow
there's no chance that time and reason will persuade
the determined abide by promises they've made

There must be a way, we say, at least to deflect
the annual rites we have now come to expect
the debts we owe to the dead, from our souls
we can pay in a way that is noble and bold

If ten years is too long by ten
can we say at eleven: this is when
we stop our pilgrimage of obligation
and return the rite to its rightful nation?

September 1987

SOME DETAIL

The omen: rain had dropped instead of dew;
No alarm bell had roused Nature's laws alert;
A sticky whiny misty light, no clarity;
Nervous killers wait; anxious grouchy traffic stalls.

Morning filled with ugly clouds,
shapeless blobs of muggy gray.
I remember fragments like the
weather and the sky that day.

Afternoon visions, officials, dogs, ambitious men;
Infamy woven with confusion, ashen fear and acid tears;
Somewhere in sleep someone had dreamed symbolic
    something;
Rage, compassion, surrender, revenge made mental
    rounds.

It was the night before,
or the night before that;
We leaned on the car, a late
summer dinner, midnight chat.

Can we remember the night? Recall if stars and moon
    emerged?
Did sleep slip into the fearful tissues of reflection?
Did bruised eyelids collapse in fatigue over hollow lenses?
Time changed a troubled course; a rape in mid morning rain.

What a laugh! Had we known
we'd've had much less aplomb;
We leaned on the hood of the car,
laughing; underneath was a bomb.

September 1988

ACCOUNTING TIME

I feel satisfied, I tell myself,
a pig in a pigsty, delighting in mud,
an unsold bean can, lodged on a shelf
a snowy egret, on a black sand beach.

I've touched the sword of vengeance;
I have serious lessons to teach
about murder and the fragrance
of lilacs in church. The preacher

intones about spiders and Hell,
while memories, awakened, reach
for their sources, a note, a bell,
a cry of anguish on the phone.

Do not speak of justice, I advise
myself. Generals remain in their Cone,
perhaps they suffer pain. The wise
owl in the old oak simply blinks.

I feel detached, but hardly free
these days, destined to think
of banal needs and horrid deeds;
only sixteen years have passed.

September 1992

ACKNOWLEDGEMENTS

Without the initiative of Nancy Lewis, her gentle prodding, brilliant organizing and loving nurturing this volume would not have been possible. Jennie Pittman and Heather Doyle held my hand next to the computer, did countless hours of creative editing and persevered to force the volume together. Carol Bernstein Ferry made insightful and essential editing comments that helped me sort literary wheat from cute chaff. Over the years, Jim O'Connor has reassured me by publishing some of my poems in *Capitalism, Nature, Socialism,* the journal he edits, in Santa Cruz, California. It meant a mountain.

Jim Abourezk, Alvin Duskin, Ann Janss, Larry Janss, Marianne McDonald, Philip Sharnoff, Marvin Stender, Cora Weiss, Peter Weiss, and Haskell Wexler all helped make this volume possible. They are dear friends.

Julia Sweig and Laura Yamhure creatively translated Pablo Armando's introduction. Julie Buckles efficiently marshalled the disparate elements into the assembly line of production. My family, friends and colleagues at IPS encouraged me over the years to keep writing poems. Rebecca Switzer offered enheartening comments on poems that I was unsure of, and she delicately pushed me to edit some that I thought finished. Pablo Armando Fernandez convinced me that I was a poet, years before the thought had ever occured to me that poems were something that required serious concentration; so I dedicate this volume to him, my more than friend.

ABOUT THE AUTHOR

Saul Landau is a fellow of the Institute for Policy Studies in Washington, D.C. He is also an author, filmmaker and frequent lecturer at colleges and universities. He teaches as a visiting professor at the University of California, Santa Cruz.

Among the awards received by Mr. Landau are: The Emmy, The George Polk Award for investigative journalism and The First Amendment Award (1980 and 1981, *Paul Jacobs and the Nuclear Gang*); Edgar Allen Poe Award for Best Non-Fiction Mystery, (1981, *Assassination on Embassy Row*); First Prizes at Mannheim (1971, *Que Hacer;* 1980, *Paul Jacobs and the Nuclear Gang*); Berlin and Ann Arbor (*The Jail*); and Ann Arbor (*CIA Case Officer, Song for Dead Warriors*). Awards at Cannes and Venice (1971, *Que Hacer*).